To Jean:
   Best wishes and warm regards
Peace, Joy + Blessings
   Enjoy these faces of Africa's future

A O Farqu
5/15/03

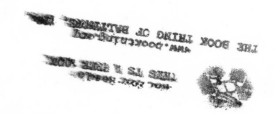

VOICES FROM WITHIN

Photographs of African Children

A. Olusegun Fayemi

COVER DESIGN:	Anne C. Pace-Rosa
FOREWORD:	Ngugi wa Thiong'o
AFTERWORD:	Ugorji Okechukwu Ugorji
TEXT AND CAPTIONS:	A. Olusegun Fayemi
PHOTOGRAPHY:	A. Olusegun Fayemi
PUBLISHER & EDITOR:	H. Donald Kroitzsh
DESIGNER:	H. Donald Kroitzsh
ASSISTANT EDITORS:	Anne C. Pace-Rosa
	Barbara A. Ritchotte

Printed and bound in the United States of America

Published for
Albofa Press
by
Five Corners Publications, Ltd.
5052 Route 100
Plymouth, Vermont 05056
USA

VOICES FROM WITHIN: Photographs of African Children
ISBN: Hardcover—1-886699-12-7; Softcover—1-886699-15-1

FOREWORD
Look Into The Eye

Colonialism in Africa was economic, political and cultural. But it was also psychological and this aspect was rooted in the images of Africa consciously and unconsciously developed by the dominating forces to reinforce economic and political bondage. For how one looks at oneself is how they look at their cultural, political, economic and natural environment. In that sense one of the worst aspects of external domination of Africa in the 19th and the first half of the twentieth century was the colonization of the image of the African. Whether in literature, in philosophy, in history or in the interpretation of the Bible, there was a constant thread of alienating the African from his own image while at the same time reinforcing the colonizer's image of Africa in order to give rational legitimacy to acts of brutality often carried out in obedience to some ethical and aesthetic ends — the colonizer's ends, of course.

One of the most persistent images of the continent in book illustrations of European adventures in the so-called "dark continent" was that of the European always at the center of action, with light radiating from him to illuminate shadowy figures of Africans who often merge with darkness. The key point here is the fact of the European being the initiator of purposeful action and the African the recipients. The other image particularly in tourist or journalistic photographic literature is that of poverty, famine and disaster. How many times have we seen that photograph of an African child with mucus on its lips, with flies massed around the nose and eyes? Or that of a starving mother and child with bones protruding, and eyes full of despair?

The picture of poverty stricken African is the other side of the coin of the exotic African wielding a spear, (oh those wonderful cultural tools!), experiencing the freedom of the wild life. So the African image oscillates between nature, fauna and flora, where he enjoys full freedom, and is the recipient of admiring attention from camera-wielding tourists, or in 'civilization' where he is the starved, diseased recipient of European charity and generosity. Dignity of poverty is highlighted at the expense of the dignity of the poor. In trying to dramatize their poverty, these images often deny the subject his/her humanity.

It is against this background that one welcomes the photographic art of Olusegun Fayemi from his earlier book *Balancing Acts*, to this second collection *Voices from Within*. Here are faces of African children from different regions of the continent in a variety of activities of ordinary living. There is nothing exotic about them and there is nothing poverty-stricken about them. They are seen in their everyday environment of changing moods and conditions. We see them playing. We see them working. We see them learning. We see them in solidarity with one another. We see them trying to cope with life. But look in their eyes. That is one of the most striking aspects of the images in this collection of photographs. Look in the eye. That look expressive of so many moods, so many memories, so many desires, but there is no despair. They may be poor, for Fayemi is not trying to hide anything, but they are of their own world and they are the tomorrow of that world. There is dignity and the drama of the poor but not the drama and dignity of their poverty. In fact, his is not a photographic essay on sociology but a simple visual enjoyment of the drama of their ordinary lives. Look into the eye and see and hear the voices from within, and they speak millions.

Behind the camera are the hands and eyes and heart of love and care. Fayemi cares for the continent and this love and care came through in the photographs of these children. His is the eye which decolonizes the African image, and I believe that in this effort he has produced a genuinely Pan African aesthetic statement. If it is true that psychological liberation can never be complete without economic and political liberation, it is equally true that economic and political liberation will be incomplete without the liberation of the collective and individual images of self. Decolonizing the African image is integral to decolonizing the mind and this collection of photographs are a part of that collective effort. But what a beauty. I can only hope that Fayemi will continue in this work and bring us many more images of the continent seen from within with the same loving and caring patience which has gone into making these photographs of African children at work and play.

Ngugi wa Thiong'o
New York

ACKNOWLEDGEMENTS

With sincerity and a deep sense of appreciation I acknowledge the contribution of many to the successful completion of *Voices From Within*. My wife, Ayodeji Bodunrin gave me unflinching support and stood by me through the vicissitude that is expected of a project of this magnitude. She always had an encouraging word, gave useful suggestions and endured, without complaint, my many trips to Africa, innumerable hours in the darkroom and long absences from home during the preparation of the manuscript.

I owe a debt of gratitude to my many guides, who protected me from crossing the line, time and time again, in my enthusiasm to photograph, and who accepted me as a fellow African brother in their respective countries. They all showed a great interest in the project, endured arduous long daily walks through the back roads of villages, towns and cities, and facilitated my acceptance by the African communities and the people I photographed. Specifically I recognize the following: Aboubacar (Senegal), Hassane (Niger), Achenef and Samson (Ethiopia), Peter (Zimbabwe), Meshack and Solomon (South Africa), Seth (Ghana) and Gormont Pierre (Ivory Coast).

I am especially grateful to Ngugi wa Thiong'o for taking the time and effort to write the Foreword, Chester Higgins Jr. for useful advice and encouraging words, to Dr. O. Ugorji for support, invaluable assistance and for writing the Afterword and a glowing recommendation for the book, Prof. Ali Mazrui for an endorsement and to Shittu Gambari for his assistance in editing the photographs. I wish to acknowledge Victor Davson, the Executive Director of Aljira, a Center for Contemporary Art, Newark, New Jersey for moral support and helpful suggestions. Finally, Don Kroitzsh of Five Corners Publications has been a gem, a true gentleman, who handled the publishing of the book with infectious enthusiasm and genuine professionalism.

INTRODUCTION

"No one continent has been more mistreated, misunderstood and misreported over the years than Africa. Ask an American to mention four things he associates with Africa and the answer is likely to be "pygmies, jungle, heat, lions." Yet pygmies have been all but extinct for decades, jungle is now as uncommon as snow in Southern California, the heat is no more intolerable than that in Washington, D.C. on a summer day, and lions are so few in number that most Africans have never seen one." *(David Lamb)*

The true and complete realities of Africa are not reflected in the Western press. Most journalists who report on contemporary Africa cannot resist the pitfall of applying western standards as the ultimate criteria for evaluating their subjects or in judging events that occur in that continent. Too frequently they fail to comprehensively examine the complex realities that constitute Africa. From their superficial impression emerge opinions, deductions and conclusions that misinterpret and misrepresent Africa and distort the realities of the continent and its peoples.

Television or print reportage about Africa is invariably negative, and usually consists of natural disasters, civil wars, political violence, massive bloodshed, despair and desperation. Totally lacking is a multidimensional overview of key issues or a fair representation of the diversity of insights that may shed light on the problems and glories of the continent.

A glaring, and definitely misleading example of distorted reportage is that in which western media presents the typical African child as hungry, malnourished, lethargic and disease-ridden: an epitome of misery and a victim of unfortunate circumstances. In their effort to raise funds, charitable organizations shock television viewers with close-up images of potbellied, emaciated children, many cachectic with skin hanging loose over flimsy skeletal frames. In these pictures, the surroundings are generally stark, bare, and devoid of any comforts of life; healthy children and adults are usually not evident.

Though these images are shown for only brief moments, they are so powerful that their effect on perpetuating a negative image of the African child persists and endures. The pictures linger in our minds and have become the standard by which African children are measured. Furthermore, most western journalists and media believe that all African children are non-descript, lack identity and are uniformly miserable and wretched.

Indeed it is true that many African countries continue to wallow in grave economic difficulties. Some have suffered tremendous economic setback in the last twenty years or so. The effort at industrialization and modernization has stagnated and, in many cases, regressed. The huge debts these countries owe the West have seriously curtailed and stymied their development and have adversely affected their economic growth.

In recent times, these problems are compounded by a particularly unfriendly international economic environment that has become less accommodative or, at times, hostile to the interests of developing countries. Running parallel with this are unfavorable terms of trade and reverse resource flow, all wreaking havoc to the economies of the continent.

Perennial massive bureaucratic corruption, chronic political instability and gross mismanagement also have contributed to severe economic downturns. Governments continue to spend hard-earned tax monies, their meagre resources, and financial aid and grants for lavish projects that have little or nothing to do with improving the quality of life of the masses. Currencies have been devalued, inflation runs unbridled and uncontrolled, and consumer prices have skyrocketed. Prolonged, sometimes vicious civil wars, associated with gargantuan population shifts have created millions of refugees and impoverished many. Additionally, natural disasters such as drought, deforestation and desertification of previously arable land have made shortages of food, undernourishment and intermittent starvation recurrent in many places.

Simultaneously, the World Bank and the International Monetary Fund (IMF) have emerged as extremely significant external influences in the economic, political and social life of almost all African countries. The IMF's demand for structural adjustment programs has meant drastic changes in domestic policies designed to ensure greater economic profitability and efficiency and a more effective integration of the economies of developing countries into the world economy. Unfortunately, these policies often generate severe strains or internal political instability, socio-cultural upheavals and severe suffering of the masses (Martin & O'Meara, Salim)

During these difficult times, children bear a disproportionate larger burden of societal deprivation and share a greater impact of its economic crises, wars, natural disasters, and poverty. Nations overburdened with debt tend to initially reduce those services that affect children the most: education, health care and child welfare. When living standards decline, infant mortality rises and malnutrition increases; when there is famine it is the children who first succumb to its devastating effect. Thus the children have become the focus of western media and charitable organizations and truly deserve all the attention that has been paid them. The largess of western governments, UNICEF and private donors have saved the lives of millions of children.

However the deep concern for the unfortunate and disadvantaged has shifted focus from those millions of African children who live relatively normal lives, even in areas of conflict, famine or other forms of human suffering. In fact the vast majority of African children belong to this category. Visible malnutrition, usually the result of war or drought or other exceptional circumstances affect only about 3 - 4% of African children (UNICEF).

The horrific pictures painted of the African child fails to take into account the remarkable progress that African countries have made in improving the lives of their children. For example, since becoming independent, 18 African countries have reduced the death rates of young children by 50% and another 35 countries by more than 33%. To put this achievement in perspective, it took Europe about 70 years to halve infant and childhood mortality rate. During the 1980's and early 1990's, African countries exceeded expectations in the percentage of their children who were immunized against common deadly infectious diseases. Now more than 15 million children are immunized annually in spite of transportation and other difficulties encountered in reaching remote locations.

In 19 countries the average level of immunization is now higher than in some industrialized countries. It is expected that many African countries would eradicate polio, eliminate neonatal tetanus and drastically reduce measles cases and deaths by the turn of the century.

The introduction and use of oral rehydration therapy (ORT) has markedly reduced the death rate from diarrheal diseases, the second commonest cause of death in young children. Dehydration, the consequence of diarrhea, can be prevented in nine of 10 cases by ORT. Other areas where significant progress has been made include reduction of subtle and moderate malnutrition, and vitamin and mineral deficiency, increased access to safe water, adequate sanitation and basic education.

Today, most African children continue to survive and thrive in spite of the adversity of the times and the gloomy prediction about the future of the continent. In my travels in Africa I have watched, played and spoken with these children in all kinds of places: on city streets, in the backroads of towns and villages, in schools, learning a trade or other survival skills, doing house chores, running errands and playing mischief. In some cases, during repeated visits to a place, I have had the opportunity to watch some of them grow up and mature over several years. As I observe them I see a reflection of my childhood and adolescent years in southwestern Nigeria.

Growing up in Africa conjures romanticism and sentimentality — probably more so among those who lived their early years on that continent. Children enjoy a life, simple in its content, imbued with close family ties. Near and distant relatives of three generations or more live in the same compound or in close proximity to one another. Deep respect for elders and societal mores and customs are inviolable and unassailable. Children are taught the mystery of spirits and reverence for ancestors. Additionally there is the excitement and challenges of living in two worlds, the one indigenous and ancient, the other western and modern.

Voices from Within is a book of photographs of children from Africa south of the Sahara. It celebrates the lives of ordinary children and their every day life: how they are nurtured and reared, the games they play, their adolescence and growing up years, their education and their role within their families and immediate environment. These photographs reveal the essence of the African child and do not resemble the familiar image that the outside world has come to associate with him/her. And yet these are the prevalent and most common images that jump at one as one walks through the high density areas of Accra, Harare, Addis Ababa, Bamako, Nairobi or through the streets of less well known places such as Tubulolo (Ethiopia), Aiyede (Nigeria), or Adeiso (Ghana).

In these photographs one gleams that happiness of most children does not reside in the quantity of material things they or their families possess. In my conversations with children all over the continent, once the parents or guardians are able to provide love, a few changes of clothes, adequate meals and shelter, the thought of poverty (particularly as defined by non-Africans) seem far from their minds. In fact, the concept of material deprivation does not begin to occur to most African children until their late preteen years. Thus the casual and superficial observation of visiting journalists who do not live the African life or their readers who interpret static images as representational of the spirit of the African child is, false. To be able to appreciate the lives of African children, the photographer or writer needs to walk the streets extensively, live with the people, play with the children and have almost unlimited access inside the homes where the children live.

Africa is as complex as it is interesting. To understand Africa takes more than a casual visit to the continent, more than a fleeting television "bite" of a few seconds and definitely more than the jaded view of some political commentator or social scientist. Many of these "experts" tend to measure Africa by the only standards they know — those of industrialized nations of the world. They often quote statistics (often slanted) to bolster their views, opinions, and conclusions.

In fact the image of abject poverty, despair, misery and wretchedness are often times snapshots of short periods of time in the life of contemporary Africa. They have never truly represented the essence or the realities of the continent. As once expressed by Blaine Harden, an American journalist who spent four years in subSaharan Africa, "the news from the continent that seems doomed to overpopulation, famine, and political instability is incomplete and misleading."

The photographs in this book, made over a 17 year period during which I travelled to 12 African countries, are a reflection of my experiences and my perception of the realities of African children. The images represent a realistic but warm and intimate glimpse into their lives. My growing up and being raised in circumstances similar to those of the children of today provided me the advantage of being able to relate to the realities of African childhood and the ability to understand the subtleties of their lives. Stephen Marc once observed that "exploring black heritage is important because it is insufficiently and sometimes inaccurately addressed in the American mainstream education and in Eurocentric accounts of history... it is important that black people are involved in the process of portraying and defining themselves."

The question may be raised about the objectivity of photographs which portray mainly a positive image of African children. As amply pointed out in the text accompanying these photographs, I have not ignored the difficulties African children face today; I have only attempted to document a more balanced picture of the African child in contrast to the usual fragmented and sensational images and accounts by the Western media. The images in this book are an accurate reflection of my feelings and experiences, particularly by one who has lived a similar life and who thoroughly understands the children. The work is not intended to romanticize poverty or deny the difficulties facing African children but to portray them as honestly as they are, without comparing them to children in other parts of the world.

A. Olusegun Fayemi
New York

Where You're Going

BEING NURTURED

"Since God couldn't be everywhere He (or She) created mothers ..... and fathers."

M. Konner

In Africa, a child is a special gift and a cause for celebration. Africa has a tradition of cohesive family units and a strong system of child care and protection which relies heavily on immediate and distant relatives.

The tie between the mother and child is particularly tender and strong and in most cases begins at birth. The protective process starts with breast-feeding. Later the child is strapped to the mother's back so she can perform her daily chores. With the child on the back, the mother can walk around, carry things on her head, go to the market, dance, cook — does virtually everything that she does when she is not carrying the child.

In his observations of children and their mothers in an African hospital, Dr. Collis commented: "Like all African mothers, they had come to stay too, for African mothers don't leave their children in hospitals. They come with them and stay beside them most of the time, feeding them, doing some of the nursing, and above all giving them confidence and security."

Breast-feeding lasts months and sometimes, years. In the first few months of life, mothers breast-feed babies several (up to 20) times a day and less frequently at night. In many parts of the continent mothers and infants sleep together at night thus facilitating breast-feeding. This pattern of nursing also assures early bonding between mother and child. Most African women are uninhibited about breast-feeding which they do even in public places such as the marketplace and other gatherings, in buses, hospitals, or by the roadside. The child is nursed on demand and no time schedule is ever kept. Nowadays, however, many women, mostly the educated and/or urban dwellers consider it improper, or are bashful of nursing their babies in public or when others are present. As is often the case in Western culture, they prefer to breast-feed privately. While children may be nursed when they seem perfectly content, nursing may be used to pacify a crying baby or to prevent a baby from fussing or throwing tantrums.

Commenting on the probable role of breast-feeding on the temperament of African children, Collis expressed his sentiment thus: "...children came along smiling without fear, presenting themselves for examination with far less fuss than children in Europe. Maybe the reason is that African children have much more security in their subconscious than ours, all being breast-fed for many months, sometimes years, and all carried on their mothers' backs till they are two or three years old. Or maybe it is because African children just have better nerves and a happier disposition than ours. Whatever the reason, Yoruba children are the most entrancing in the world."

Multiple caregiving and fostering are two unique forms of traditional nurturing. In multiple caregiving, an ancient African family tradition, the mother passes her baby around to other caregivers whose duties include feeding, cleaning, bathing and generally watching over the baby. The caregivers are usually close or distant female relatives such as grandmothers, aunts, cousins, older female siblings of the infant, and less commonly friends of the mother. Sometimes a hired young female may serve in this capacity. Caregivers arrive at the home of the newborn infant soon after the child is born and may stay thereafter for weeks to months, even years. In addition to taking care of the infant, caregivers assist the mother in many household chores. In polygamous families, co-wives may participate in caregiving duties. Under normal conditions, almost no woman is ever the only caregiver of her baby.

Young children are frequently used as caregivers. A common sight on the streets of African cities, towns and villages are children taking care of younger children. Toddlers are strapped to the backs of young female children, who themselves, are in their preteens or a little older. The process begins with mothers recruiting their older children, usually females in the six to twelve year old range, for this purpose. The child nurse most commonly is an older sibling, cousin or young aunt and may be required to feed, bathe, clean up, play with, and generally watch over their charges. Supervision of toddlers by children may last for short periods of time but may also last hours or the better part of a day.

Child nurses are usually girls; boys are chosen for this chore only if girls are not available to do the job. These nurses perform an extremely important function in the life of the family: not only do the toddlers have the full attention of their young caregivers, but the mothers also have the freedom to attend to other duties that take her away from home or other domestic or out-of-the-house chores that are incompatible with simultaneous baby tending. Although child nurses have a certain degree of autonomy in performing their nursing duties, they are expected to call an adult if some major or minor emergency arises.

Voices From Within

Multiple caregiving ensures that the infant interacts regularly with several different individuals. The child is almost never alone, even when sleeping. The child, therefore, forms multiple attachments but with the mother as the main attachment figure. This practice also provides a buffer and support system to reduce postpartum stress and depression. Further, caregivers contribute significantly to the infants' social and mental development in the first year of life.

After weaning, it is a primary responsibility of parents to see that their children are adequately fed and nourished. Diets vary in quality and quantity from place to place, and this, in part determines the proportion of children who will be malnourished. Carbohydrates form the staple and mainstay of most diets; protein in the form of fish and meat are consumed much less than in industrialized countries. In times of food shortages, adults will limit their intake to assure adequate food for their children.

African mothers take care of most of their children's physical needs in the first few years of their lives: feeding, protection from physical dangers, toilet training, training in proper hygienic behavior, and complying with the norms of their culture. Mothers also instruct their children, especially girls, in skills that are necessary for handling household chores and appropriate and acceptable social behavior.

African fathers play only a minor role in the lives of their infants and toddlers. The participation of multiple caregivers, comprising mostly of women, limits the involvement of men in the nurturing of children in their early years. However, there are rare societies like the Kung of southern Africa where fathers have intimate and close interaction with their infants and toddlers. Fathers become more involved with their children when the children are past infancy — in late childhood and adolescence. Some men will play with, feed, bathe, and supervise their children; fathers who are educated also assist their children with their school work and assignments.

It is in the area of discipline that the father becomes a central figure in the life of the African child. In many African societies, mothers depend on their husbands to discipline the children; often mothers threaten to, or actually do, report incidents of children's misbehavior to their husbands for the latter to mete out the appropriate punishment because mothers find it difficult to control youngsters, especially boys. In cultures where mothers discipline their children, fathers are usually the stricter disciplinarians.

Children are expected to be deferent and respectful, and, sometimes, submissive towards their fathers; fathers are not only the head of the household but, in most instances, also retain the economic power over the family. This relationship between fathers and children lasts a lifetime, even when the children are grown and economically independent.

Closely related to multiple caregiving is fostering, a custom particularly common throughout West Africa. Parents send their children to live with other more affluent or more educated relatives, who usually live in an urban area, until the children reach puberty or early adulthood. It is an excellent mechanism for spreading the cost of feeding and clothing children. The children, in turn, perform domestic chores or assist in the commercial enterprise of their patrons. This practice provides the children with greater access to educational opportunities because their surrogate parents live in urban areas where schools are more plentiful and varied; the children also benefit from the higher economic status of their benefactors, who are expected to send them to school or provide the opportunities for apprenticeship in some vocation such as automobile mechanic, carpentry, petty trading, dress making, metal works and the like. Over the years, the bond between the patrons and foster children becomes as strong as that between parents and their biological children.

The customary nurturing of the African child occurs regardless of the economic condition of the family or community. In fact the family bond and ties become stronger in times of need and deprivation. The legendary resilience of the African in the face of adversity (civil wars, drought, population shift, etc.) may, in part, be due to the strength of character and the unselfish spirit imparted during his or her nurturing.

Mother and Child. Addis Ababa, Ethiopia, 1997

3

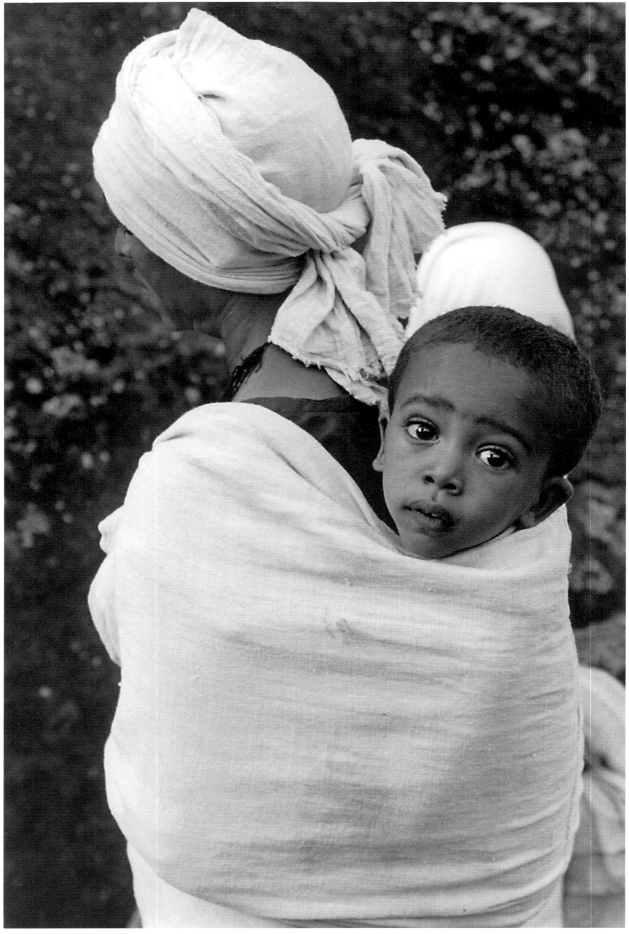

Mother and Child at prayer time. Lalibela, Ethiopia, 1997

Weaver and child. near Ifaki Ekiti, Nigeria, 1981

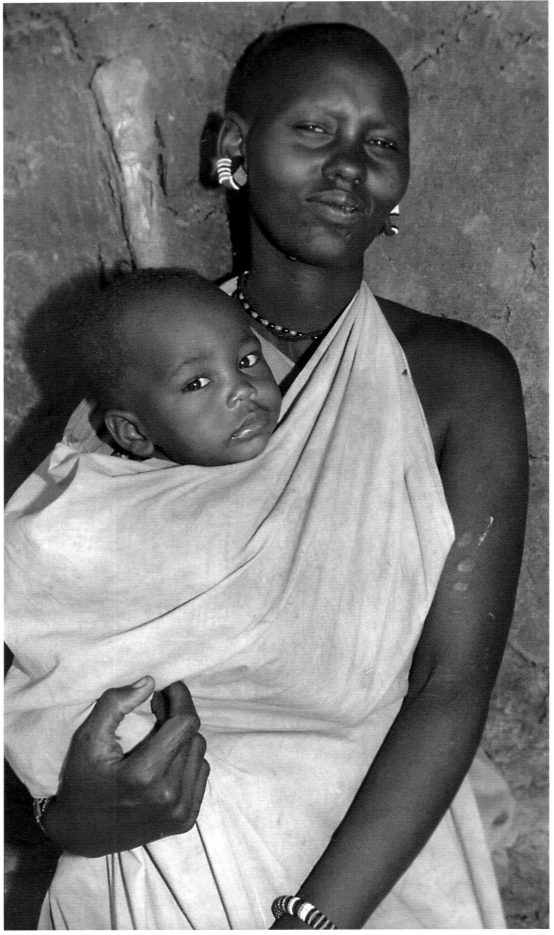

Mother and Child. Masai village, Kenya, 1994

Sisters. Decamhare, Eritrea, 1997

Voices From Within

Sisters. Addis Ababa, Ethiopia, 1997

Young caretaker. Jaji, Nigeria, 1982

Caring for younger brothers. Dakar, Senegal, 1992

Brothers. Soweto, South Africa, 1996

Bucket bath. Harare, Zimbabwe, 1996

Helping mama. Harare, Zimbabwe, 1996

Twins. Soweto, South Africa, 1996

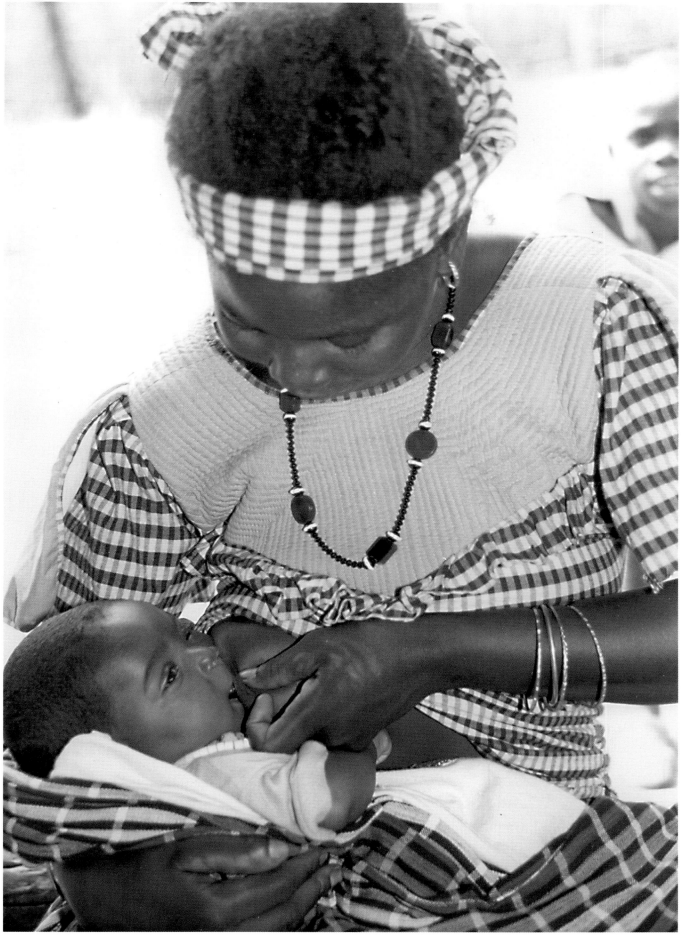

Meal time. Nguoye Diaraf, Senegal, 1992

Meal time. Lalibela, Ethiopia, 1997

Meal time. Loyangalani, Kenya, 1994

Early morning river bath. Mopti, Mali, 1993

Mother and children on the banks of River Niger. Ayorou, Niger, 1995

Bucket bath. Ifaki Ekiti, Nigeria, 1982

With grandmother. Addis Ababa, Ethiopia, 1997

Father and children. Lalibela, Ethiopia, 1997

Father and son. Lalibela, Ethiopia, 1997

Mother and son. Lalibela, Ethiopia, 1997

Mother and children. Abidjan, Ivory Coast, 1992

Mother and son. Aburi, Ghana, 1996

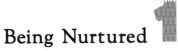

Meal time. The child prone on the mother's lap is being fed corn meal. Ile Ife, Nigeria, 1983

27

Mother and child. Mombassa, Kenya, 1994

2

IN SEARCH OF KNOWLEDGE

"The greatness of the human personality begins at the hour of birth. From this almost mystic affirmation there comes what may seem a strange conclusion: that education must start from birth."

Maria Montessori

Across from St. George's Hotel in the Adabraka section of Accra, Ghana lies a Methodist elementary School accommodating a few hundred students. By 7:30 am school children, all dressed in uniforms, scurry around performing cleaning chores: sweeping litter from the school yard and classrooms, cleaning the wall blackboard in preparation for the first class of the day; other students huddle around trying to complete their homework. A teacher is in attendance to supervise these activities. A number of food sellers are perched on rocks and small stools in service to multitudes of students who buy and eat their breakfast at school. The sound of the school hand bell summons all the students to the school yard where, a few minutes later, they line up according to their classes and in descending order of their heights. Following announcements, prayer and pledge to the flag, the students march in an orderly fashion into their classrooms. So begins the average day in most elementary and secondary schools all over Africa.

On the way to Decamhare in Eritrea, high school students bicycle their way over steep hills in the sweltering early morning sun on their way to Asmara, some twelve miles away. There are other students who walk many miles from remote villages over rocky and rough unpaved terrain to the highway and then ride in public transportation to their schools.

The thirst for education is unquenchable; most families recognize the value of and the advantages that formal education confers on the individual in the African society and would stop at nothing to provide the means for their children to go to school. Success at school is important to parents who understand that the child's occupational advancement depends on it. Basic education, which involves instruction in literacy, numeracy, life skills and critical thinking, helps children become self confident, improves their productivity and promotes tolerance for ethnic, religious and cultural differences.

The statistics support the significant progress that has been made in the basic education of African children. Today over 80% of school age boys are enrolled in grade one of primary school, double the number that enrolled in 1980.

During the same period, girls' enrollment in primary school quadrupled. Although elementary school completion rates vary and average just less than 50% in subSaharan Africa, there are some countries where a high percentage of students complete four years of primary school. For example, Zimbabwe graduates 94% of its primary school students, just a shade less than the 96% reported for developed countries. (UNICEF)

Progress has also been made in reducing the gender gap in primary school education. Whereas only one third of enrollees were girls in the early 1960's, that ratio has increased to about 50% in the 1990's. However, gender differences and discrimination become quite marked in secondary and tertiary education. In the former, the enrollment for boys and girls are 22% and 11% respectively. The gender gap is at its worst at the tertiary level of education where enrollment of women is only about 1.5% of that of men. Girls have always been and continue to be at a disadvantage when it comes to education. To illustrate, during family economic difficulties, girls are more likely to be withdrawn from school than boys. However, efforts are being made by many national and international organizations to encourage parents and governments to support the education of women.

Although there is a considerable improvement in primary school enrolment, drop out rates continue to plague the educational systems across the continent. In order to reduce dropout rate, it has been suggested that the quality of education must be high and cost be low. The former would increase the demand, improve motivation among students and teachers and encourage parents and communities to support with money and material towards the cost of maintaining schools. Further, education must be practical and marketable so that parents can better appreciate the need to subscribe to the concept of formal education. After all, in the short term, families benefit financially if the children work for money rather than attend school.

The curriculum needs to combine core subjects focussed on basic skills with optional subjects adapted to the social context, local job markets and to the religious and cultural aspiration of the community (UNICEF). Subjects taught should be linked to primary health care (including AIDS prevention, nutrition and immunization), family planning, agricultural and economic development and peace (respect, tolerance and non-violence). More effective education programs and better classroom techniques have also been advocated. Among other key principles, UNICEF advocates that educational needs should reflect African realities and traditions. European primary and secondary school models may not be appropriate in certain circumstances and should be modified accordingly. Community involvement in the educational process also assures greater chance of success and may allow literacy programs to be extended to adults.

African schools teach not only academic subjects – mathematics, science, reading, writing etc. – but also arts and crafts (basketry, pottery, metal works and the like), gardening, agriculture, husbandry and home economics. Students actually participate in the maintenance of the school buildings and yard and their surroundings. Sporting activities, most commonly soccer, track and field and table tennis complete the school world of the African child.

Religious instruction and education, either Islam or Christianity, constitutes an integral part of formal education in parochial and some private schools. Children also receive instructions in the tenets of Islam and the study of the Holy Quoran in after-school classes — especially those who attend non-Muslim schools. In some parts of West Africa, there are children whose sole formal education consists of the study of the Holy Quoran. Christian education takes the form of the study of the Holy Bible in preparation for baptism, first communion or acceptance as full members of the church.

The introduction of European education has led to a marked decline in traditional education especially in urban areas where modernization, westernization and the availability of modern technology are prevalent. Education in indigenous traditions and mores have become weak, simplified and distorted. It is not uncommon to find children who cannot read, write or speak their indigenous language with any proficiency and some who cannot eat many local foods. Western values and culture are sometimes so alluring that they obstruct children and their parents from assimilating their own indigenous culture. Historically these problems emanate from the colonial school systems that left little or no room for instruction in African history, culture and traditions. Independence has done little to improve this deplorable state in many parts of Africa. However, many countries and communities are making efforts to redress this situation and have had to reeducate Africans in their own culture.

Clearly, the formal setting of the classroom or the school yard is not the only way African children acquire education. In many rural and remote areas formal education is scant or nonexistent. Traditional African education was aimed at the harmonious integration of the individual into the society. The child was taught the techniques necessary for individual and community life as well as the nonmaterial aspects of the culture. Although no generalizations can be made for the multitude of ethnic groups in Africa, in most instances the first stage of traditional education during the first three years of life was, and sometimes still is, the mother's responsibility. After weaning, young boys and girls are educated by their older siblings and then increasingly by adults, at first within the family circle and later in a broader sphere that may include house chores, farming, herding and some trade or craft.

Learning takes many forms. Children are taught handicrafts and gain practical knowledge that will serve them in their future lives. Girls learn how to prepare meals, general home care and how to care for younger siblings. Boys learn to tend herds and grow crops. Both are taught money-making skills that will benefit the family.

When serving an apprenticeship, the child is as much a servant as a learner. He is bonded to a master of a craft, trade or profession and is assigned to the master's care. During the period of apprenticeship, the child is expected to do menial, sometimes dangerous work, relating to the chosen avocation. The craft is learned slowly over time, usually years, until the apprentice is "freed" and has become a proficient and accomplished craftsperson. Carpentry and cabinet making, stone masonry, auto mechanics, cloth weaving, commercial automobile driving, food selling are some of the crafts or trades that may be studied in this fashion. Apprenticeship demands rote repetition, authoritarian teaching and chore assignment and is observative and interactive. (Konner)

The most visible apprenticeship, seen on the streets of most African cities, is that of young men (and adults) who serve as assistants to drivers of public commuter buses (called by different names including 'bush taxi', 'matatu', 'car rapide', 'molue', 'kia kia'. They invite passengers to their buses by yelling out their destinations as the buses ply the roadways, seat their clients in available vacant seats, collect fares from passengers, and generally serve as the "eyes" and "ears" of their bosses, the driver, who then is able to concentrate and devote his full attention to driving in the overcrowded, often-times, dangerous roads.

In the African society of today, vocational education and apprenticeship for learning a skill or trade have their places. However, if children are truly going to be the future of Africa, greater effort must be made to expand and improve the curriculum of formal schools at all levels to reflect the fast pace required to compete in the 21st century. While the industrialized countries enjoy the benefits of the tremendous advances of modern technology — computer, space exploration, engineering feats, internet etc. — African countries must make a serous effort to uplift themselves from the incessant distraction of civil wars, political instability and corruption. Examples abound of countries that have made a remarkable transformation within a few decades from a state of underdevelopment to becoming industrial giants. These countries have demonstrated that "miracles" can occur with proper national focus and unwavering, single-minded policies that concentrate on the education of their masses, including children. Many of these countries achieved their success while maintaining their indigenous national and cultural characteristics. Africa must focus on the education of its children so as to be in a position to effectively compete in the 21st century.

Kindergarten class, Mary Immaculate School run by the Franciscan Sisters of the Poor, Parcelles, Senegal, 1992

Kindergarten class, Good Shepherd Nursery School, Nairobi, Kenya, 1994

Open air classroom. Epworth, Zimbabwe, 1996

Quoran class. Dakar, Senegal, 1992

The Imam and Islamic students. Goree Island, Senegal, 1993

Studying to become a cleric. Lalibela, Ethiopia, 1997

Boys studying the Quoran in an Islamic school. Accra, Ghana, 1996

Reading a story together during class break. Harare, Zimbabwe, 1996

Voices From Within

Break time. Asmara, Eritrea, 1997

Returning from school. Soweto, South Africa, 1996

Returning from school. Asmara, Eritrea, 1997

Children's library. Soweto, South Africa, 1996

Student Council, Madibane High School. Soweto, South Africa, 1996

Classroom, Seipateng Primary School. Diepkloof, Soweto, South Africa, 1996

Voices From Within

Lunch time. Soweto, South Africa, 1996

Buying lunch. Soweto, South Africa, 1996

School band, New Hope School. Accra, Ghana, 1996

Palm Day Parade, New Hope School. Accra, Ghana, 1996

Morning assembly, Methodist School, Adabraka. Accra, Ghana, 1996

51

Telling African traditional stories and tales to students. Harare, Zimbabwe, 1996

Homebound after school. Soweto, South Africa, 1996

Returning from school. Soweto, South Africa, 1996

Voices From Within

Returning from school. Epworth, Zimbabwe, 1996

55

After school hours. Asmara, Eritrea, 1997

Cooling off. Epworth, Zimbabwe, 1996

Doing homework. Soweto, South Africa, 1996

Doing homework. Ifaki Ekiti, Nigeria. 1983

Doing Homework. Aburi, Ghana, 1996

Altar boys. Abidjan, Ivory Coast, 1996

3

AT HOME & WORK

"I started rearing a few chickens which I sold for six pence each. By this means I could not only help to meet the school fees, but I had money to buy books as well."

Kwame Nkrumah

"The child shall not be admitted to employment before an appropriate minimum age; he shall in no case be caused or permitted to engage in any occupation or employment which would prejudice his health or education, or interfere with his physical, mental or moral development. "
(United Nations Declaration of the Rights of the Child)

Monilola, a 10 year old bright pretty girl, lived with her uncle in an upper middle income section of Ibadan, a sprawling city of several million people in southwestern Nigeria. She would wake up at about six o'clock in the morning to begin her daily domestic routine, which included sweeping the living room and kitchen, fetching water from a water tank outside the house for cooking and bathing, dusting the furniture and assisting her aunt in the kitchen during the preparation of the family breakfast. She would find time to take a bucket shower, dress for school and wash the breakfast dishes, all before 7:30am, when her uncle's chauffeur or one of the car-poolers in the neighborhood would drive her to school located four miles away. She would return from school at about 2:00pm and before dinner, would play for a short time, but then would do some more kitchen and cleaning chores. She would still have time to put in more than two hours of school- and home-assigned home work. By the time she went to bed at 10pm she would have spent no less than four hours assisting in a variety of domestic chores.

A child of similar age coming out of a less affluent family would still do similar tasks but may spend more hours doing them. She may have to walk to school, assist her mother by taking care of her younger siblings, may sit at her mother's shop after school hours while her mother goes to the market or engages in some other economic activity or she may have to go out to hawk a variety of wares on the streets.

Nearly all African children, regardless of their economic status, actively participate in domestic work. Children from upper income and wealthy families do much less because there are hired hands such as maids and cooks who are employed to do most of these household chores. Children are incorporated into the family work force early in life; many spend much of their time each day doing serious work. Even those who attend school are expected to do their chores before and after school hours. Most of the time, doing chores, whether at home or out of the home, is regarded as a necessary part of growing up. Children's participation in domestic chores not only is necessary in non-technological, agrarian or pastoral societies but it is also believed that the practice builds character, instills discipline and prepares the child for a productive adult life in the community.

At home, girls do more chores than boys. From as early as five years of age, girls may have begun to supervise their younger siblings while their mothers are at work either at home or away from home. Children fetch firewood and water, grind grain, onions, pepper, beans or pound yams and the like; they also cook or assist in cooking meals. Cleaning chores such as sweeping, dusting and throwing out garbage are usually relegated to children. Boys assist in many manual aspects of farming — hoeing, making heaps, planting, weeding, and harvesting. They also care for animals, large or small. It is always fascinating to watch the contrasting picture of small-statured preteen boys guiding large herds of cattle for grazing. Babalola (1996) succinctly described the role of children in household work thus: "Some time was allowed for doing homework but it was a bounden duty for us to lend a hand in the kitchen with chores, contributing to the cooking of the supper..... The pounding of fermented maize grains in a mortar for the preparation of maize starch and the pounding of skinless dried unripe plantain slices .... were common chores for boys. The girls were involved in grinding chores, vegetable picking chores and water fetching."

In addition to doing household tasks, children also make serious and important contributions to the economic welfare of their families. Often this takes the form of direct financial contribution as is evident in those children who work at subsistence tasks. These jobs require considerable responsibility by the children from which they build life-long economic skills.

Assisting with household chores and participating in activities that improve the economic welfare of the family need to be distinguished from what has been termed exploitative work. At times there is only a thin line that separates these two phenomena. In recent times child labor has become the focus of attention in both industrialized and developing countries. Although child labor may be interpreted in dissimilar ways by different countries and cultures, the International Labor Organization has enunciated the salient features of exploitative child labor as distinct from children working in socially and personally useful ways. In broad terms, exploitative child labor occurs when children are put to work or are allowed to work like adults at an early age, when they work for small wages, when they work under hazardous and dangerous conditions or conditions which hamper their health and personal mental and physical development.

The work done by some African children may be classified as exploitative. Examples of such labor abound on the streets of many African cities. Children work for upwards of twelve hours a day as apprentices on public transportation systems; they sell food and non food items during daylight hours at traffic intersections and motor parks; they are seen manning roadside malls and many engage in full time petty trading. Most of these children do not attend school and many spend their early years doing these tasks. In fact some are "street children" who are truly homeless.

Parents teach and demand responsibility from their children. The training begins as early as three or four years of age when children are sent on minor errands. Older children are expected to perform more demanding and a larger variety of tasks. For example boys begin to herd animals and girls may go fetch water from the spring or river. Children who fail to live up to their responsibility are often scolded or punished. Responsibility training is stressed more for girls than for boys; for example, girls are incorporated into tasks such as nursing and supervising their younger siblings or cleaning the house at a much earlier age than boys.

The widespread availability of modern technology on the continent has significantly reduced the amount and changed the type of physical tasks African children perform. In urban and semi-rural areas, the availability of electricity, even for just a few hours a day, means that grain can be ground at mills instead of pounding or using grinding stones, clothes can be ironed with an electric iron instead of a coal-fired iron; easy access to public transportation has eliminated long walks to and from school or market; food can be cooked on gas or electric stoves obviating the need for fetching or cooking with firewood; the availability of potable water, either at home or in the neighborhood, eliminates walking long distances to fetch water.

African children are taught to show respect to their parents and those older than them, including older siblings. In many African societies, respect to elders takes the form of outward deference in the spoken word and physical demonstration such as bowing to, or prostrating oneself or kneeling before the older person. Children must use respectful language when addressing their elders, and when being scolded, they cannot demur or contradict their parents. Indeed, in many African societies, children are to be seen and not heard. Children are usually not asked what they think of issues nor can they offer their opinions spontaneously.

Obedience is regarded as a virtue in practically all African societies. Parents demand it from their children; older members of the family from younger ones. Relative age dictates the tone of relationship between individuals, with the younger people deferring in a variety of ways and contexts to older ones. Elders are also the keepers of cultural traditions and may not be questioned by children or young adults.

Disobedience and irresponsible behavior are frowned upon and incur disciplinary action, often physical. Parents may flog their children or administer some other form of corporal punishment. In his autobiographical book of his childhood, Soyinka (1981) painfully but eloquently described some types of corporal punishment administered to children in southwestern Nigeria thus, "...this world of beatings, facing the corner, 'stooping down', which required that the culprit stand on one leg and raise the other and stoop over forwards, resting one finger on the ground. The other arm was placed penitently on the curved back. Another favorite punishment was standing up with arms outstretched, parallel to the ground. The cane descended sharply on the knuckles of the miscreant if either arm flagged, just as, in stooping, an attempt to change the leg earned the offender severe strokes on the back."

Caning was the commonest form of discipline in years past, but the practice did not create cries of child abuse. In schools, teachers used the cane freely and liberally as punishment for a variety of offenses such as lateness to school, failure in academic work, failure to do one's homework, disrespect to the teacher, fighting and raucous behavior in class and moral failings such as stealing or cheating during class tests. Although caning is still a popular form of discipline in many places, it appears that urbanization and modernization have led to a dramatic decrease in this form of punishment. After all, African children can now be punished by being denied television watching and other "pleasures" of late twentieth century in modern Africa.

I do not want to create the impression that the world of the African child comprises continuous work and not much else. And although corporal punishment is employed to discipline children, this happens less frequently now than a few decades ago and the average child may pass through his/her childhood without once being spanked. Furthermore, there exists African societies where corporal punishment is almost unknown, or, when they do exist, is mild. As a rule, African children grow up in an atmosphere of love, caring and support from their nuclear family and the immediate and distant relatives.

In the upper window. Lalibela, Ethiopia, 1997

Voices From Within

Front yard. Ayorou, Niger, 1995

Hawking groundnut oil. Ibadan, Nigeria, 1981

Hawking home-made brooms. Ilorin, Nigera, 1982

Hawking sugarcane. Ibadan, Nigeria, 1981

Mending fishing net. Lagos, Nigeria, 1992

Selling clay pots. Ilorin, Nigeria, 1983

Young petty traders. Harare, Zimbabwe, 1996

Boy weaving basket. Esure Ekiti, Nigeria, 1983

Domestic chores. Adeiso, Ghana, 1996

Children selling wares at motor park. Ilorin, Nigeria, 1983

Running an errand. Abidjan, Ivory Coast, 1996

Apprentice tailor. Mopti, Mali, 1993

Grinding grain. Lalibela, Ethiopia, 1997

Sieving cassava flour. Ayorou, Niger, 1995

Picking chaff out of corn seeds. Addis Ababa, 1997

Pounding for fun. Addis Ababa, Ethiopia, 1997

Apprentice carpenter. Dakar, Senegal, 1993

Kitchen chores. Asmara, Eritrea, 1997

Voices From Within

Young herdsmen on the Niger River, near Niamey, Niger, 1995

Boy with cassava stems. Adeiso, Ghana, 1996

Voices From Within

Going to fetch water. Loyangalani, Kenya, 1994

Firewood. Lalibela, Ethiopia, 1997

Laundry day. Soweto, South Africa, 1996

Bucket bath. Ifaki Ekiti, Nigeria, 1982

Bucket bath. Ilorin, Nigeria, 1981

Bucket bath. Ibadan, Nigeria, 1981

Cooling off. Aburi, Ghana, 1996

4

Fun & Games

"Not so the children...For them there are open spaces and fenced-in compounds on the corner where they play running games. They chase one another with sticks. They kick a ball around the patch of dirt surrounded by overhanging trees. It is a serene existence."

Eddy L. Harris

The clock strikes five o'clock in the afternoon and the sun is hanging low in the horizon. A few wispy fair weather clouds gather loosely against the blue sky. The sleepy and languid streets of the early steamy afternoon awake from their lethargy and come to life. Adults return home from their work place; children, having rested from their day at school or the farm emerge and begin to spill on to the streets; petty traders, mostly women, spread their wares for sale in front of their houses; food sellers set up wood, kerosene or coal stoves to start a long evening of cooking and selling. With increasing intensity, the human traffic swells and the milling masses gradually fill the streets to enjoy the cool breeze and obtain some respite from the trapped heat in their houses. Most noticeable are the children found all over — on the sidewalks, playgrounds, porches and verandas, and indeed, in the middle of the streets engaged in all sorts of games and play — street soccer, jackstones, card games, running games, jumping games and pretend games.

This scene, typical of rural or urban Africa repeats itself everywhere south of the Sahara: from Adabraka in Accra, Ghana, to Surulere in Lagos, Nigeria, from Mbare in Harare, Zimbabwe to Treichville in Abidjan, Cote d'Ivoire, from Diepkloof in Soweto, South Africa to Loyangalani in northern Kenya.

Like children the world over, games and play are central in the life of the African child. As a child growing up in southwestern Nigeria in the forties and fifties, I have vivid and fond memories of a life full of fun and adventure and the joys of exploration of my environment. My earliest recollections are those of watching older children and young adults fashion toys and playthings from whatever was available: wood, strings and ropes, metal pieces, paper and sand. Young children would sit for hours on end watching with rapt attention while the older ones built and fabricated toys with intricate and superb details. These toys provided endless hours of amusement and pleasure. By itself, the process of making these toys was pure joy. As I grew older, I participated in these activities — making wheeled toys (sometimes one could not tell nor did we care whether they were cars or lorries), practical and magical stringed and wind musical instruments, kites,

spinning tops, sling shots, to mention just a few. These childhood experiences are similar to those of other children all over Africa.

Most African children do not have access to toy stores or electronic games. Even in the cities where such facilities may exist, most families do not have the financial resources to indulge in these forms of entertainment. But this has not deterred children from spending active, exciting, merry and lively periods of relaxation and play. Surely play time for the African child is far from boring or uninteresting. He has always resorted to his creativity and ingenuity to fabricate games or playthings. Any and all things can serve as toys or can be used to make toys. For example, Joseph Lijembe from Kenya observed, " we would make use of simple materials, sand, soil, bricks, stones, string, sticks, bottles, banana balls, banana ends, hoops, maize cobs, baskets, certain grasses, green branches, catapults, bows and arrows and drums" Similarly, on the joys of exploration of one's environment as part of fun and games, Kwame Nkrumah wrote: "It was a wonderful life for us children with nothing to do but play around all day. Our playground was vast and varied, for we had the sea, the lagoon, and the thrill of unexplored bush all within easy reach."

In my travels in Africa, I always saved empty film canisters to give to children to play with. Invariably they are excited by these seemingly useless plastic containers. I often wondered what they did with them. From my experiences of growing up African, I was sure that these containers were put to good use and probably last a long time. My suspicions were confirmed when, on a visit to Ayorou in Niger (a six-hour bus ride from Niamey, the capital), I gave these containers to the children of my host, the headmaster of the only high school in town. About half an hour later, the children had placed millet seeds in the containers and had turned them into a rattle, which, when shaken rhythmically, provided appropriate accompaniment to their melodious songs.

For most children it is the pure joy of playing that keeps their interest for hours on end. Some games such as street soccer, board games, jacks are designed to be competitive and the spirit of winning rather than playing is strong.

Voices From Within

However, that desire is generally not strong enough as to diminish the fun derived from playing the game.

Many of the games that African children and adults play are known in virtually every part of the globe and have existed for centuries, some dating back to the preChristian era. Such games are universal and have transcended cultural, racial or linguistic barriers; many have spanned enormous distances in time and space. For example evidence exists that children of ancient Greece, around 500 BC, played with spinning tops, hoops and toy wagons; Chinese children of more than 1000 years ago played pretence games, rode hobbyhorses and played blindman's buff; European children in the sixteenth century have been depicted in pictures that show them in many types of familiar modern games such as jacks, rolling the hoop and pretend wedding. It can only be conjectured whether these games arose as a result of imitation and influence from other parts of the world or come from independent invention of children living at opposite ends of the globe but who have similar inventiveness and fantasy.

A strong relationship exists between some games and African indigenous religions, customs or rituals. Some of such games are relics often dating back centuries earlier and sometimes are a crude imitation of these rituals; in others, the significance of playthings go deeper than the mere joy the children derive from them. For example the Asante dolls called akua'ba not only serve as playthings for girls but also are used to protect pregnant women. Similarly tossing jacks at the beginning of that ubiquitous game is reminiscent of Ifa (Yoruba) divination practices and the associated ability to tell fortunes and forecast the future.

Certain games foster and nourish intellectual development while others sharpen and maintain physical skills. The famous mancala games with its multiple variants (wari, oware, ayo, adi, walu, hus, to mention just a few) have been played for thousands of years in Egypt and occur in innumerable local forms throughout Africa, the Caribbean, the Philippines, Asia and South America. It has aptly been called "the game played by kings and cowheads — and presidents too". One of the oldest games in the world, it is played by adults in intricately and ornately carved wooden boards and by children in holes scooped out of the earth using pebbles or seeds as counters. The game is highly complex and demands fine mathematical calculations of possible moves and their results in which the objective is for each player to capture as many of the 48 seeds used in the game as possible. When adapted to the computer, it has been suggested that the number of possible advantageous moves in a game numbers more than 400,000! (Zasvalasky)

Draught (checkers), a board game which originated in Europe, about the beginning of the 12th century, also requires sharp intellectual skills and quick thought processes. African children improvise both boards and "men" as the need arises. Bottle tops, square cut wooden "men" and hand-cut cardboard pieces are a few of their adaptations. The children still adhere strictly to the rules of the game and, in spite of the simplicity of the board and pieces, derive uncountable hours of fun from the game. Other board games played by two or more children, usually boys, are table soccer, achi-achi (Ghana), a modified type of pin ball.

Several games such as tiddley winks, racing the hoop, foot races, hopscotch and kite flying demand physical strength, dexterity, coordination or marksmanship or a combination of these skills. Somewhere in their growing-up years, most African children, particularly boys, would have raced or walked the hoop. There are all kinds of hoops: small or large, rubber or metal, adapted from bicycle tires or wheels or fashioned from car tires. It is always fascinating to observe small children racing wheels almost as tall as they are. When children are sent on errands by their elders, running the hoop provides an avenue for expeditious completion of these tasks because the children run to and from their destinations. Occasionally competitive races are arranged by the children themselves to determine who can run the fastest with their hoops.

Hopscotch, which originated during the Christian era, and which is thought to symbolize the journey of the human soul from earth to heaven, is a popular game with children all over the world. In Africa boys and girls of all ages play many variants of the game whose objective is to project a stone or marker onto a marked diagram on the street, concrete pavement or dirt and hop in specific patterns without touching any of the lines. The diagrams or court are usually outlined with chalk, crayons on the pavement or with a stick on the ground. The game can be played by two or more children who take turns in a regular order. The winner is determined by the player who had gone through the entire game with the fewest number of misses.

Street soccer (football) is the most common game boys play. A relatively clear space or streets that have scanty or no vehicular traffic is all that is needed. The goal posts may be as simple as two rocks spread apart or may actually be as sophisticated as goal posts with a net when the game is played on a soccer field. The soccer ball varies from a small used tennis ball to a standard leather soccer ball; in between there are rubber balls of varying sizes. In places the ball may be homemade, usually of an assortment of material admixed with rubber which gives the ball its bounce. The neighbors, passers-by, bicycle and other vehicular traffic coexist peaceably with the children through unwritten rules of respect for one another. Adults have learned over time to accept as part of life the noise that accompanies the game as well as balls falling on their roofs or yard and the dusty atmosphere created by the players. When I was growing up, this was virtually the only game adolescent boys played — and we played it barefooted!

Excitement and plenty of raucous behavior mark the game of marbles, usually played by two or more boys with several more hanging around as interested spectators. This is a game of marksmanship, physical control, eye and hand coordination and strategy and is played with glass or plastic "marbles". Relatively more sedate than street soccer, the game is most popular among older adolescents.

"Pas temp" is a guessing game in which two girls face off, clapping, jumping and twisting their bodies to the rhythm of a short song at the end of which one leg is thrust forward. One player is a designated leader and the other the challenger; the latter is supposed to guess which leg

the leader would thrust forward. The game continues as long as the challenger correctly guesses the leader's moves. When the challenger falters, she is eliminated and another contestant jumps in to continue the game. This goes on until all the girls present have had a chance to face off with the leader. Though quite physical, girls may play this game for hours on end. The rules of the game are similar in all West African countries.

The genre of games involving tricks or solving puzzles encompasses cat's cradle and egg jousting. Since eggs can be expensive and difficult to obtain by children, walnuts may be substituted for eggs. Nighttime games, particularly moonlit nights, are common during the dry season. Hide and seek games, running and clapping games, singing and dancing are among games and activities that provide fun for African children. Sometimes children sit around adults who tell them stories about their ancestors and the mysteries of nature and life. Riddles and proverbs which concentrate on wisdom of the elders, morals and ethics are integral to these nighttime activities.

Water games. Abidjan, Ivory Coast, 1992

Jackstones. Dakar, Senegal, 1993

Art on sand. Harare, Zimbabwe, 1997

Vast playground. Accra, Ghana, 1996

Somersaulting. Goree Island, Senegal, 1992

Upside down. Yoff, Senegal, 1992

Pull! Harare, Zimbabwe, 1996

Posing. Adeiso, Ghana, 1996

Jumping game ("elastic"). Abidjan, Ivory Coast, 1996

Draughts (checkers). Harare, Zimbabwe, 1996

Pretend kitchen. Abidjan, Ivory Coast, 1992

Jumping rope. Lalibela, Ethiopia, 1997

Schoolyard games. Harare, Zimbabwe, 1996

On the swing. Epworth, Zimbabwe, 1996

Climbing. Niaga, Senegal, 1992

Running the hoops. Accra, Ghana, 1996

Relaxation. Accra, Ghana, 1996

Playthings (wheels). Accra, Ghana, 1996

Home made car. Fana, Mali, 1993

Cat's cradle. Abidjan, Ivory Coast, 1996

Guessing game. Addis Ababa, Ethiopia, 1997

Dexterity. Ayorou, Niger, 1995

Aware. Soweto, South Africa, 1996

Aware. Adeiso, Ghana, 1996

Street soccer. Dakar, Senegal, 1992

Marching band. Soweto, South Africa, 1996

Doing the high jump. Aburi, Ghana, 1996

Table soccer. Dakar, Senegal, 1992

On a tricycle. Lagos, Nigeria, 1982

ELOQUENT FACES:
GROWING UP AND MAKING FRIENDS

"O happy, happy time of childhood, never to be recalled!
How could one fail to love and cherish one's memories of it?
These memories refresh and elevate my soul and are for me the source of all my best pleasures."
Leo Tolstoy

With a population of about 800 million and more than eight hundred distinct ethnic groups, Africa presents an ancient, complex and diverse traditional society, with a mosaic of values and culture. Parallel to this complexity, childhood, adolescent and growing up experiences in Africa are varied and diverse. This enormous diversity in Africa means that childhood experiences vary from country to country, ethnic group to ethnic group; they also vary according to geographic location within the continent, location within a country — coastal, in the hinterland, in the savannah, desert or forested areas or whether the child lives in a city or rural area. They also may vary according to the economic status of the child's family or community — rich, middle class or poor, or according to the religious background — Christian, Moslem or most uncommonly, traditionist.

The passage of time has also had profound effect on growing up African. Contemporary African history has witnessed the partition of Africa into countries with artificial geographic borders over seven decades of European colonization and more than 30 years of independence. The introduction of western values and modern technology to indigenous African peoples, as well as the teachings of Christianity and Islam have had a dramatic impact on traditional African life and beliefs which, over time, has affected the growing up process of the African.

Under these circumstances of innumerable cultures combined with the external factors, particularly Western values, no single description of typical African childhood is possible. Nonetheless, childhood in rural Africa was, and in many cases, still is, serene and tranquil and has certain universal common characteristics of which the most important is psychological security fostered by closely-knit family ties and a warm, friendly and supportive community. As observed by David and Harrington, " the African tribal childhood had a secure beginning. He was born into a non-industrialized society which, in comparison with contemporary society, was relaxed and personalized. He was a member of close-knit group and had a definite place in a clearly defined universe."

In many African societies the life cycle phases of puberty and adolescence are marked by transition rituals called the rites of passage (such rites are also performed during life's major transitions — childbirth, marriage, parenthood and death). These ancient and symbolic practices make demands on the individuals in an attempt to impress on them the appropriate code of conduct and behavior within the community.

These rites of passage give children a stronger subjective purchase on adulthood which symbolically is represented by the pain and psychological stress associated with these rituals. Once the rituals are completed, the initiate feels that he/she is a part of something, in this instance, part of the culture and the community. He/She feels a strong affinity and pride in belonging to the world of adults as distinct from those yet to be initiated. New initiates are permitted to participate in various adult activities and rituals, some spiritual. The initiation process serves as a forum for the transmission, through formal instructions, of specific cultural practices and the roles expected of the typical adult in that society. The rules governing the behavior of the individual in the society are also emphasized.

Puberty or adolescent rites of passage or formal recognition of these developmental milestones are not universally observed among all Africans. About one third of ethnic groups do not or only minimally acknowledge this period in the lives of young boys and girls. Even in areas where the practice takes place, there is a higher fraction of initiation in the adolescents who live in rural areas than those who reside in the cities. Girls are also more likely to undergo the initiation rites than boys.

For boys, initiation rites take the form of psychological and physical challenges, circumcision and less commonly, some form of hazing. For girls it means learning cultural norms of cleanliness such as correct disposal of menstrual blood, learning the roles of a woman at home and in the society and, among some groups, clitoridectomy. Some ethnic groups espouse fattening for fertility as an important part of the initiation. In these societies, the ideal woman is plump to such a degree as to show creases at the neck, for which she is judged to be healthy, beautiful and fertile.

Making friends is central to the growing up process. Friendship among African children is similar to that of children in other societies. When children are young, play groups may be mixed by age or sex. However, as they grow older, they tend to segregate themselves into same-sex groups and may even go on to form special friendships with particular individuals. Parents usually prefer and actively encourage same-sex friendships among older children in order to avoid premature sexual entanglements. Friends play, eat together and may sleep together in each other's house.

Early on, children's friends are drawn from immediate or extended family members who live in the same compound or in close proximity to one another. Parents encourage children to stay around the house and not stray too far from home; naturally this limits the number of possible friendships that the children can make. When children begin school, their circle of friends enlarge to include nonrelatives.

Play and games form the central focus and the major bond of friendships at a young age. Youngsters usually gather together in late afternoon, early evening after school or after they would have finished their household chores. They form groups or pairs to engage in a variety of playful activities such as street games, running and jumping games, wrestling, card games, street soccer and the like. Some friendships continue beyond the playground into other areas of the child's life such as the school, the church, or the mosque, particularly when the friends are the same age and attend the same school.

Many friendships continue to adolescent years and beyond. Some last a lifetime and the children of friends may also become friends. In elementary and secondary schools with boarding facilities the close proximity which characterizes the living arrangements sometimes promotes strong and lasting friendships among children who have had the privilege of this kind of education. In many such schools, students live together in dormitories, eat at the same time in cafeterias or dining rooms, play sports together, study together, and attend classes together for weeks at a time without returning home. These circumstances provide a fertile setting for the development of lasting relationships.

Loyangalani, Kenya, 1994

Mombassa, Kenya, 1994

N'gor, Senegal, 1992

Voices From Within

Soweto, South Africa, 1996

Soweto, South Africa, 1996

Decamhare, Eritrea, 1997

Addis Ababa, Ethiopia, 1997

Voices From Within

Parcelles, Senegal, 1992

Yoff, Senegal, 1992

Goree Island, Senegal, 1992

Soweto, South Africa, 1996

Soweto, South Africa, 1996

Mopti, Mali, 1993

Addis Ababa, Ethiopia, 1997

Asmara, Eritrea, 1997

Abidjan, Ivory Coast, 1996

Dakar, Senegal, 1993

Addis Ababa, Ethiopia, 1997

Decamhare, Eritrea, 1997

Loyangalani, Kenya, 1994

Epworth, Zimbabwe, 1996

Soweto, South Africa, 1996

Soweto, South Africa, 1996

Niaga, Senegal, 1993

near Zaria, Nigeria, 1983

149

Jaji, Nigeria, 1982

Soweto, South Africa, 1996

Lalibela, Ethiopia, 1997

Loyangalani, Kenya, 1994

Accra, Ghana, 1996

Goree Island, Senegal, 1992

Lalibela, Ethiopia, 1997

Lagos, Nigeria, 1982

BIBLIOGRAPHY

Babalola, S. A. (1996): *More than Conquerors.* Lagos: Advent Communications Ltd

Balander, G.; Maquet, J. (1974): *Dictionary of Black African Civilization.* New York: W. Morrow and Company

Black, M. (1993): *Street and Working Children.* Innocenti Global Seminar. UNICEF

Broude, G. J. (1995): *Growing Up. A Cross-Cultural Encyclopedia.* Santa Barbara: CLIO-ABC

Collis, R. (1967): *In Africa is People - First Hand Account from Contemporary Africa* (editor Nolan, B.) New York: E. P. Dutton

David, J.; Harrington, H. (editors) (1971): *Growing Up African.* New York: W. Morrow and Company

Ennew, J.; Milne, B.: *The Next Generation. Lives of Third World Children.* Philadelphia: New Society Publishers

Fox, L. K. (editor) (1967): *East African Childhood - Three Versions.* Nairobi: Oxford University Press

Grunfeld, F. (editor) (1975): *Games of the World.* New York: Holt, Rinehart and Winston

Harris, E. L. (1992): *Native Stranger.* New York: Simon and Schuster

Hodjar, K. B. (1990): *Africa in an Era of Crisis in "Western Journalism and the Third World"* Trenton: Africa World Press

Konner, M. (1991): *Childhood.* Boston: Little Brown and Company

Lamb, D. (1987): *The Africans.* New York: Vintage Press

Marc, D. (1992): *The Black Trans-Atlantic Experience. Street Life and Culture in Ghana, Jamaica, England and the United States.* Chicago: Columbia College

Martin, P. M.; O'Meara, P. (1995): *Africa, 3rd edition.* Bloomington: Indiana University Press

Montessori, M. (1969): *The Absorbent Mind.* Translated by A. Claude. New York: Dell Publishing Company

Nafzinger, E. W.: *Inequality in Africa. Political Elites, Proletariat, Peasants and the Poor.* Cambridge: Cambridge University Press

Nasan, D. (1985): *Children of the City. At Work and at Play.* Garden City: Anchor Press/Doubleday

Nkrumah, K.: *The Autobiography of Kwame Nkrumah*

Opie, I. and P. (1969): *Children's Games in Street and Playground.* Oxford: Clarendon Press

Patel, M. (editor) (1995): *Atlas of the African Child.* UNICEF

Salim, S. A. (1992): Opening remarks in *Culture and Development in Africa.* Proceedings of International Conference. Washington D.C.

Soyinka, W. (1981): *Ake. The years of Childhood.* New York: Random House

The Dragon Group (1975): *The Way to Play.* New York: Paddington Press

Tolstoy, L. (1964): *Childhood, Boyhood and Youth.* Translated by M. Scammel. New York: McGraw Hill Inc

Zavalasky, C. (1973): *Africa Counts.* Boston: Prindle, Weber and Schmidt Inc.

AFTERWORD

While engaged in my daily pursuits of life, liberty and prosperity in America, I had forgotten those happy, simple days of my childhood in Africa, at Lorji-Mbaise in particular. I had forgotten the nakedness of my black skin under the peculiar heat of the African sun and the teasing gales that often came from the Sahara. I had forgotten growing up in huge compounds that made orphanages unnecessary for centuries in Africa. I had forgotten mimicking contests with birds that I always lost. Tucked away also were the memories of weekly road clearings with adults; the fetching of water from the Nri River and Giri-giri Nwanjoku spring. How about moonlight seminars on morality disguised as storytelling sessions! I had forgotten, that is, until I saw the photographs in Olusegun Fayemi's Voices From Within: Photographs of African Children.

In Voices From Within, we see through the eyes of one who was in the same shoes of his subjects, one who is perhaps still in the same shoes. Stubborn images of the present that easily fool one to think they were from years gone. Splendid images that grab you and seem to be proclaiming aloud, "But of course I am African and I am a child." These are voices from within. The title of this collection at once speaks to the scores of faces with several stories to tell, and at the same time to the voices within Fayemi himself. The children and the author, through their voices, sing our ethos. They showcase our motif. They reveal our politics. They share our religions, and they apostrophize the reader on the subject of who we really are: the progenitors, the sun people, those made in the image of God.

As I started off saying, I thought I was doing well in America until I saw the orgy of happiness in these photographs. These images also challenge all of us of the African world. How could one wage war in the midst of such beauty? How could leaders hide away billions of currency in European and Arabian banks at the expense of the children in these images? How could we allow the devastation of the environments in which these children reign? How can we continue to justify the second class citizenship of the women who gave birth to these children? How, these voices ask! How!

Fayemi must be praised, honored and celebrated for this extravagant ode and pictorial poetry dedicated to the African child. In accomplishing this authoritative and majestic presentation of the African child, the author presents all of humanity - indeed our griots tell us that all humans are Africa's children. I find in this work a homeostasis of voices that culminate into a brilliant orchestra of gumption in imagery and a mastery of the photographic arts. There has never been a greater exhibition of the quintessence of the human spirit than one sees in these images. Like the Ifa priests of antiquity, Fayemi has deified our essence in this work. The ancestors must be proud, and generations to come will be grateful for Fayemi's Voices From Within.

Ugorji Okechukwu Ugorji, Ed. D.
Author of From the Belly of the Gods.

A. OLUSEGUN FAYEMI

Born in Ifaki Ekiti, southwestern Nigeria, Olusegun Fayemi spent his childhood, formative and early adult life in Nigeria. He studied photography privately, with Alex Harsely and Richard Sternschuss of New York and at the New School for Social Research, International Center for Photography and Zone VI studios. For the last 18 years he has focused on, and directed his energies to, social documentary photography of continental Africans and Africans in the diaspora. This project provided him the opportunity to travel extensively in Africa, the West Indies and the United States. His photographs have been published and exhibited widely in the United States, Nigeria and Hong Kong and are included in many public and private collections. He is the author of *Balancing Acts*, a critically acclaimed and widely successful book of photographs from West Africa (Sungai, Princeton, 1995).

When not making photographs he practices Medicine as a pathologist and Director of Laboratories at the Franciscan Health System of New Jersey.